BY MORNING

OTHER BOOKS BY SERPENT CLUB PRESS:

What Was Left of the Stars
Claire Åkebrand

Circumambulate
Daniel Bossert

A Quarter Century
Eda Gasda

Moon on Water
Sonata for Piano and Violin
Matthew Gasda

Autumn, Again; Spring, Anew
Michael Skelton & Stephen Morel

The Substitute
Michael Skelton

On Bicycling: An Introduction
Samuel Atticus Steffen

AND OUR JOURNAL
New Writing: Volume I
New Writing: Volume II

BY MORNING

An original drama by Matthew Gasda

SERPENT CLUB PRESS

BY MORNING
Copyright © Serpent Club Press, 2017
All rights reserved

First Edition

Printed in the United States of America
Set in Williams Caslon
Designed by Emily Gasda

ISBN
9780997613438

BY MORNING

BY MORNING had its world premiere at Rockwell Studios in Brooklyn, New York, opening on March 7th, 2017 (Charlie Munn, Producer). It was directed by Matthew Gasda; the set design was by Axelle Dechellete; the costume design was by Melissa Nelson; lighting design was by Joseph Medeiros. The cast was as follows:

Logan...........................Michael Johnson
Gabriel........................... Charlie Munn
Dylan ....Tad D'Agostino
Iris .... Maeve Crispi

Characters:

Logan, *a former football player; lawyer, 27*
Gabriel, *an actor, 25*
Dylan, *a successful entrepreneur, 23*
Iris, *Logan's high-school sweetheart, 26*

Logan, Dylan, and Gabriel are brothers from a close-knit family; Logan, though he grew up with Dylan and Gabriel, is a half-brother from their father's first marriage

Setting:

Living room of upper middle-class family home in the suburbs.

ACT I

Dylan, Logan, and Gabriel sit quietly in a semi-circle in the living room. A bottle of whiskey is open on a coffee table.

The brothers wear black suits. They sit solemnly, very still.

LOGAN
Fuck fuck fuck fuck fuck fuck fuck.

GABRIEL
I don't know what to do.

LOGAN
Fuck fuck fuck.

DYLAN
I think I'm gonna go…

LOGAN
Why?

DYLAN
I can't stay in this house. I'm gonna find a hotel.

GABRIEL
Sit the fuck down.

DYLAN
Lay off.

LOGAN
It's one night. One night, Dylan—and then you can go back to doing whatever the fuck it is you do. Write financial algorithms and suck your own dick—

DYLAN
You don't need to insult me to make your point.

LOGAN
Sit. Down.

DYLAN
I don't want to be here anymore.

GABRIEL
You can't run away from it…

DYLAN
You're such a sanctimonious prick—

GABRIEL

I'm serious.

DYLAN

Yeah so am I: I need to get away from here. Like, right now.

LOGAN

If you walk out that door right now, don't think about coming back.

DYLAN

Logan...

LOGAN

The three of us need to talk. Like really talk. About it.

DYLAN

What's there to say? Some dickhead chose to blow himself up in the lobby of Mom and Dad's hotel. And now they don't exist. There: we talked about it. Now can I go?

LOGAN

You're running away—

DYLAN

I'm putting an end to this farcical bonding experience—

LOGAN

Coward.

DYLAN

It's easy for you to say Logan, you still have a mother—

GABRIEL

Dylan...

LOGAN

Dude—

DYLAN

I'm serious: it's a significant difference between us. Your biological mother exists, ours doesn't.

LOGAN

Do you hate me Dylan?

DYLAN

No.

LOGAN

Because it seems like you do.

DYLAN

What I hate is pretending like I have a relationship with either of you.

GABRIEL

But you don't pretend.

DYLAN

What I'm proposing is that we bury the flawed idea of family along with our parents—

GABRIEL

You're bitter.

DYLAN

I'm not bitter, I'm realistic.

LOGAN

You're bitter.

DYLAN

I don't see the point in honoring a life that was hell for me. I mean, it was a lot for me just to come to the funeral.

LOGAN

Don't exaggerate.

DYLAN

You're proving my point for me. I'm constantly being browbeaten; cut off, belittled, commanded—

LOGAN

I'm not—

DYLAN

Yes you are—

LOGAN

You just don't like being called out—

DYLAN

You're trying to do this whole thing where you assume the mantle of patriarch; but...you're, like, a joke.

LOGAN

Thanks.

DYLAN

You're welcome.

LOGAN

Fear of Dad's disapproval has formed my entire life.

GABRIEL

So why are you acting like him?

LOGAN

Because he trained me to replace him once he was gone. My programming's kicked in.

GABRIEL

I think Dad was so hard on you because he thought you were the only one who actually loved him.

LOGAN

I didn't love him, I feared him; obeyed him—

GABRIEL

Which he registered as love—

LOGAN

He tested my loyalty every single day, because I guess he didn't trust it. He secretly felt like a fraud. A fraud father. So he punished me for it.

DYLAN

Wah wah wah wah wah. You poor baby.

GABRIEL

He's trying to express himself—

DYLAN

We didn't grow up talking about feelings, so it seems inappropriate to start talking about them now.

LOGAN

Those aren't feelings, those are facts.

DYLAN

Facts about feelings—

LOGAN

It's deeper in me than I know. That programming. It's survived in me. Which means: he's survived in me. Shit. Fuck.

GABRIEL

Anxious. I feel anxious.

DYLAN

Have you tried pharmaceutical drugs? They're wonderful.

GABRIEL

Every time my phone buzzes, my heart starts to race. And I know that lightning isn't supposed to strike the same person twice, but it's so hard not to feel vulnerable to everything now.

DYLAN

Would you be upset if I died Gabe?

GABRIEL

Yes.

DYLAN

I don't see why.

GABRIEL

Because I would.

DYLAN

Aw, do you love me Gabe?

GABRIEL

Reluctantly—

DYLAN

I just farted.

LOGAN

What's wrong with you honestly?

DYLAN

Whose idea was it to serve baked beans at the reception?

LOGAN

I wish you could be a normal human being for once—

DYLAN

What's more normal than having the farts?

LOGAN

I mean, emotionally—I wish you could show some dignity—

DYLAN

In other words, to be more like you: manly, tortured, torn apart by noble grief.

LOGAN

My eulogy fucking sucked. I need you guys to acknowledge how bad it was.

GABRIEL

It wasn't bad—

DYLAN
  Then what do you call it?

LOGAN
  Yeah, then what do you call it?

GABRIEL
  Sincere.

LOGAN
  Sincerely awful—

GABRIEL
  But at least you had the guts to do it.

LOGAN
  I had the guts to throw up all morning—

GABRIEL
  But you got up there and spoke—

LOGAN
  Wept—

DYLAN
  Like a baby—

LOGAN
  For twenty minutes—

GABRIEL
  It was moving—

LOGAN
  It was embarrassing—

GABRIEL
  Why do you think it was embarrassing?

LOGAN
  Because I couldn't hold it together—

GABRIEL
  So what?

LOGAN
  So what? He would've wanted me to hold it in.

DYLAN
  So what?

LOGAN
  So I hate myself.

GABRIEL
So Iris is coming over later, by the way—

LOGAN
Wait, what?

DYLAN
Oh that's actually hilarious…

GABRIEL
I invited her…

LOGAN
Gabriel-angel-of-God—

GABRIEL
She texted me!

LOGAN
Why?

GABRIEL
She wanted to share her condolences—

LOGAN
Why wasn't she at the funeral?

GABRIEL
She just found out—

LOGAN
I don't see how that's possible—

GABRIEL
No one told her!

LOGAN
What about the internet?

GABRIEL
I don't know dude!

LOGAN
But why is she coming over?

GABRIEL
Because I don't think it should just be the three of us in this house tonight.

LOGAN
I disagree.

GABRIEL
There needs to be an objective perspective—

LOGAN

Her perspective is not objective—

GABRIEL

Let me rephrase: outside perspective—

DYLAN

She's not that either—

GABRIEL

Ok ok ok. But someone who isn't us—

DYLAN

That's a pretty low standard.

LOGAN

Gabe—are you trying to fuck my high-school sweetheart?

GABRIEL

What? No, no, no—

LOGAN

That's the only explanation I have for why you invited her over here tonight.

GABRIEL

I already told you Logan, because I think she can help—

DYLAN

How?

GABRIEL

By getting us—

LOGAN

She doesn't get us—

GABRIEL

Probably better than anyone else does, actually—

LOGAN

I don't want to see her.

GABRIEL

Yes you do.

LOGAN

You're using grief—my grief—as an excuse to get close to her—

GABRIEL

No, listen to me—

LOGAN

As an excuse to try to—

GABRIEL
Logan—
LOGAN
You want to fuck the shit out of her—
GABRIEL
No that's not it—
LOGAN
I'm not an idiot.
GABRIEL
You're acting like one.
LOGAN
You're as bad as Dylan—
GABRIEL
I'm trying to help—
LOGAN
You think inviting Iris over so that you can fuck her is helping the rest of us?
GABRIEL
That's not what's going on dude—
LOGAN
Bullshit. You want to bang her. You're all about banging her. Bang bang bang.
GABRIEL
You're being paranoid.
LOGAN
Ghost—she's a ghost—I've got enough—send her back.
GABRIEL
Dude—
LOGAN
I don't see why it can't just be the three of us. Sitting here. Sharing a few glasses of whiskey.
DYLAN
Because we have nothing to say to each other.
LOGAN
We have everything to say to each other.
DYLAN
We have conventional things to say to each other.

GABRIEL
What's conventional about this Dylan?

DYLAN
Us. This. Men drinking because they can't communicate.

GABRIEL
We're not that drunk.

DYLAN
We're getting there.

LOGAN
You don't think we can communicate?

DYLAN
I mean, we're saying words.

LOGAN
How would you define actual communication Dylan?

DYLAN
That's an excellent question—

LOGAN
Well?

DYLAN
Maybe actual communication doesn't exist—

LOGAN
Then how can you blame us for not being able to do it?

DYLAN
I'm blaming us for trying, not for failing. The failure is inevitable.
The trying-in-the-first-place-part is not.

LOGAN
You really don't wanna be here; huh—

DYLAN
No.

LOGAN
Why?

DYLAN
I've already told you!

LOGAN
No, but really—

DYLAN
There's no 'but really'—

LOGAN
You're a bad liar—

DYLAN
I'm an amazing fucking liar.

LOGAN
You're an amazing fucking asshole—

GABRIEL
We're being disrespectful—

LOGAN
Speaking of disrespectful: I don't want Iris here. I'm serious.

GABRIEL
She's already on her way—

LOGAN
Tell her to turn around—

GABRIEL
No.

LOGAN
Do you wanna get punched in the face?

GABRIEL
Sit down.

LOGAN
You're gonna call her right now and tell her she's not welcome.

GABRIEL
Where did this mob-boss personality come from? Like, are you threatening me? Are you threatening her?

LOGAN
I haven't talked to her in ten years; she broke my heart. And it's still broken. And you know that.

GABRIEL
I'm sorry, but. Yeah. Call her yourself if you don't want her to come.

LOGAN
Remember when you were fourteen and I caught you jacking off outside my bedroom door while Iris and I were—

GABRIEL
Please don't bring that up—

LOGAN
It's sick Gabe. You have a sick obsession with her.

GABRIEL
I was fourteen and she was hot.

LOGAN
You went too far. And you're still going too far.

GABRIEL
Iris and I are friends—

LOGAN
What? Since when?

GABRIEL
We both live in the city. I've run into her a couple of times. We've gotten a couple drinks together.

LOGAN
Oh so you're currently fucking her and that's what this is about.

GABRIEL
No. I said we're friends. And that's God's honest truth.

LOGAN
Then why haven't you told me about this 'friendship' until now?

GABRIEL
Because look at how you react—

LOGAN
I know you've fucked her.

GABRIEL
No, listen—

LOGAN
You have—you're a worse liar than Dylan—

GABRIEL
Calm down.

LOGAN
No—

DYLAN
Here's an idea: you both want to bang her, so, why don't you take turns tonight? Tag team it. Or better yet, since this is all about measuring manhoods, why don't you both whip your dicks out and let her choose, once and for all, which one she wants to suck more?

GABRIEL
You're both mischaracterizing my intent here. The fact is, Iris is someone who cares about us; like, she's a good person—

DYLAN
What does that even mean? 'Good'—

GABRIEL
It means she wants to help.

LOGAN
She doesn't belong here.

GABRIEL
She's been in the car for several hours at this point, I can't ask her to turn around.

LOGAN
Fine. Whatever. Just don't be surprised if I don't feel like talking to you for a few years.

DYLAN
Gabe, the fact is, what you did was incredibly selfish.

LOGAN
Thank you Dylan. Out of nowhere with the assist.

GABRIEL
I still don't know why we're fighting.

DYLAN
What else is there to do?

GABRIEL
Shouldn't all this have brought us together?

LOGAN
You would think so, but apparently not.

DYLAN
Maybe if we admit that our love for them was tenuous at best, then we can really have a conversation.

LOGAN
No, see, that's your vision of our family Dylan. It wasn't tenuous, the love. Not for me. And not for Gabe.

DYLAN
Oh come on. Dad: a tyrant, Mom: psychotic—

LOGAN
Oh don't exaggerate—

DYLAN
  Fucking fool—
LOGAN
  You went to a fancy school, studied philosophy, smoked a
  lot of joints, tried to impress girls with your knowledge of
  Schopenhauer, and then decided it was time to learn how to code
  and make a fuck ton of money.
DYLAN
  Don't you think it's in poor taste to show so much petty jealousy,
  on a night like tonight?
LOGAN
  Things come easily to you because you don't feel anything,
  especially remorse of any kind.
DYLAN
  Blah blah blah.
LOGAN
  You sit there making fun of us for having feelings for Iris, but like,
  I mean, are you a virgin Dylan? Because I wouldn't be surprised.
  You're probably one of those guys who needs to finger-fuck a girl
  for three hours because you can't get it up.
DYLAN
  Are you done?
LOGAN
  So smug, so self-satisfied.
GABRIEL
  We're creating ill-will—
LOGAN
  There's always been ill-will.
DYLAN
  Do you really think I can't get it up?
LOGAN
  How would I know?
DYLAN
  Because that's never been a problem for me.
LOGAN
  Cool.

DYLAN
I don't know if you know what was like growing up with you as a brother—

LOGAN
No, I don't.

DYLAN
It sucked.

LOGAN
Well, I apologize then.

DYLAN
You soaked up sunlight, choked everything else out. Gabe managed to survive the way a fern grows under a tree; but I couldn't even manage that. I was a little clump of moss, growing in a place where the sun never hit.

GABRIEL
It's amazing how quickly we forget that we're still wearing the suits we wore to the funeral.

LOGAN
No one's forgotten anything.

DYLAN
Are you sure about that?

LOGAN
Yes.

GABRIEL
I need to get drunker than I currently am. Shit.

LOGAN
So do I.

DYLAN
I'm gonna call a car now.

LOGAN
Why are you so uncomfortable?

DYLAN
Being here is pointless. Please let me leave.

LOGAN
Look, Dylan, you're a grown man, I'm not going to stop you—

DYLAN
That wasn't your attitude ten minutes ago.

LOGAN
You've broken my will.

GABRIEL
You're not gonna leave, you just want to feel like you have the option.

DYLAN
Probably.

GABRIEL
We need to give love when called upon to give it. We can't shy away from it.

DYLAN
Are you referring to the present moment?

GABRIEL
In general—

DYLAN
So idealistic—

GABRIEL
Well—

DYLAN
Well what?

GABRIEL
It's the whole story, from start to finish. Love. There's nothing else worth repeating, nothing else worth writing down.

DYLAN
I wish I hadn't wasted my fart, because I would have loved to follow up that thought with a good ripper—

GABRIEL
I think you secretly agree with me.

DYLAN
I genuinely loathe the unwritten rule you both seem to adhere to, that every minute of our lives has to count for something higher. All it does is force us to stamp out the fires of despair with senseless rationalizations.

GABRIEL
I spent a lot of today looking at old pictures—

DYLAN
What's your point?

GABRIEL

Only love gives consciousness to memory. The love that nourishes us Dylan, the love that I'm only beginning to understand.

DYLAN

I genuinely do not in the slightest know what you're talking about.

LOGAN

I still half-expect to see Dad tomorrow: sitting under the lilac tree in an old sweater, the morning paper on his lap, a cup of black coffee in his hand.

GABRIEL

Are we gonna sell the house?

LOGAN

It still smells like them.

GABRIEL

I know.

LOGAN

Everything is them. You reach out, you reach out. And they're not there. They no longer occupy the space they carved out in the world.

GABRIEL

Jesus.

LOGAN

What?

GABRIEL

I just. Oo. It just really hurts. It's like this...sting.

LOGAN

I know.

GABRIEL

There was hope, always hope, or something enough like it to constantly astound us: as if we were always rediscovering the stars. But now there's only this self-abolished fire: something we made up, and then stopped believing in.

DYLAN

Hey Gabe: how do you endure being so unsuccessful? How do you endure audition after audition without getting any parts? Waiting tables, living in a hole—

GABRIEL

Why are you asking me a question that is calculated to hurt me?

DYLAN
Because it feels good.

GABRIEL
Mom called me that morning, from the hotel—

LOGAN
What did she say?

GABRIEL
She said that she and Dad were having a nice time. And that they were going downstairs to have breakfast.

DYLAN
What a thrilling last minute on earth!

LOGAN
Shut the fuck up.

GABRIEL
It was two in the morning for me, when she called. But I wasn't asleep and she knew that I wasn't asleep because I'm never asleep. A problem I inherited from her, incidentally.

LOGAN
I don't think we're gonna see much of each other, after tonight, are we? Maybe just at holidays.

GABRIEL
Does it have to be like that?

LOGAN
Not necessarily—

DYLAN
But it will, because that's exactly what we want: to go separate ways and to not look back.

GABRIEL
We're alive, we're alive, we're alive. We should do something about it. We can change. We can wake up tomorrow, changed—

DYLAN

We either bury bodies or burn them—and the purpose of both is antiseptic. Rotting bodies stink and carry diseases. We shouldn't forget that: that the funeral rituals are about cleansing. It's wiping down the counters, scrubbing the floors. Dying is an evolutionary necessity, objectively speaking, without it, life on this planet wouldn't be possible. Our hearts are programmed with a specific number of maximum possible beats for a reason. I work with a lot of dudes in tech who want to reprogram their biology so that they can live for another hundred years, or another thousand, or like, forever. But I hardly need to explain that these are the most petty, delusional, self-absorbed human beings on earth. It really annoys me that the word futurism is associated with this like, turn-yourself-into-a-computer utopianism. Like what exactly is appealing about a world filled with immortal tech jocks? It's like, people are paying a lot of money to have their heads chopped off and frozen after they die, because they actually think it'd be fun to wake up again in some alien future where nothing they recognize or loved exists or is even remembered. Science was supposed to be a reprieve from religion, but it's turned out to be the same thing: an attempt to shatter time and bring back the dead. I think actually our civilization is indistinguishable from ancient Egypt, where corpses were stuffed with sawdust and myrrh. Only now we promise to transform neurons into silicon tubes. Promise. As if death isn't programmed into everything. As if life had a destination other than oblivion. It isn't, it doesn't. What are we really upset over tonight? Our parents lived longer, more comfortable lives than 99.9% of people who have ever lived. They lost a few years off the top. They didn't suffer. And the years they lost, they would have spent being mummified by modern medicine. Like, do you ever see old people in parks, in wheelchairs, pushed by caregivers, totally incapacitated, and wonder what the point is of keeping bodies alive like that? Miserable, shrunken husks; alone, abandoned, tormented. Why? What's the point? I mean, why do we fetishize life to the point where we don't know how to end it? I dunno. Like, why bother with self-improvement, changing yourself, transforming yourself...when you can't get at the basic programming that's gonna stop your heart one day soon?

GABRIEL

Dylan—man—I want talk to you, I want to know you—

DYLAN

Uhuh.

GABRIEL

I don't want to just get stuck in this cycle of insult and injury—

DYLAN

You're not gonna get to know me. Not now, not ever.

GABRIEL

Why?

DYLAN

Because, what is there to know?

GABRIEL

You—

DYLAN

And who's that?

GABRIEL

You tell me—

DYLAN

I don't know any better than you do.

LOGAN

I pours the whiskey. I drinks the whiskey.

DYLAN

Our moral grace is exhausted—

LOGAN

Speak for yourself—

DYLAN

We're going in circles—

GABRIEL

No, tell me Dylan—what do you mean by that?

DYLAN

There's no lesson to be learned here. There's no truth to take with us as we set back out along the road of life—

GABRIEL

When did I say there was?

DYLAN

It's the premise implicit in everything you're saying—

GABRIEL
You get the sense doing Shakespeare that he was a very good, patient listener; that nothing about human beings bored him—so I think that's why I keep going to auditions—

DYLAN
That's nice.

GABRIEL
You must really loathe yourself.

DYLAN
Duh.

LOGAN
Is Iris really on her way? Is that a real thing?

GABRIEL
Yes, I already told you.

LOGAN
Rat, rat, rat, rat, rat: I smell a rat.

DYLAN
Hey, I think this is the first day in a decade where I haven't looked at my phone. My brain feels almost clean.

GABRIEL
Tonight reminds me of that big storm that hit the house when we were teenagers and knocked the power out—

LOGAN
Dad listened to baseball on a transistor radio, Mom read by candlelight—

GABRIEL
We played hide-and-go seek with all the neighborhood kids; and it was great because the whole block was completely dark and spooky and dripping with rain water and littered with broken branches...I'm hungry, is there any food in the fridge?

LOGAN
There are a ton of leftovers.

Exit Gabriel.

DYLAN
Please don't try to make small-talk with me—

LOGAN
Ok...

DYLAN
The world is a terrifying feedback loop, don't you think?

Enter Gabriel, with a plate of food.

GABRIEL
I didn't realize how hungry I was.

LOGAN
I still haven't gotten my appetite back.

GABRIEL
Sorry…

LOGAN
No, don't worry about it.

GABRIEL
I can't believe I'm stuffing my face like this—

LOGAN
You're hungry, why feel bad?

GABRIEL
Are you sure you don't want some of this?

LOGAN
Yeah, I'm sure.

DYLAN
I'm gonna go get a plate.

Exit Dylan.

LOGAN
You know he won't eat anything that someone else has touched, right?

GABRIEL
I feel bad for him.

LOGAN
Which is what he wants: our secret sympathy—

GABRIEL
I don't know about that—

LOGAN
He's manipulative—

GABRIEL
He's unhappy—

LOGAN

Unhappy people are manipulative people.

GABRIEL

Is it that simple?

LOGAN

Yes. Actually. I know from experience.

Dylan returns, with food.

DYLAN

Talking about me?

GABRIEL

No.

LOGAN

Yes.

DYLAN

I figured.

LOGAN

It wasn't anything terrible—

DYLAN

What did you say?

LOGAN

You're so sensitive.

DYLAN

Is that a problem for you?

LOGAN

No, is it a problem for you?

DYLAN

Yes, it is.

GABRIEL

We're all sensitive. Clearly.

DYLAN

I'm really looking forward to getting on a plane and getting the fuck out of this family.

LOGAN

I'd love to beat the shit out of you.

DYLAN

Why don't you then?

LOGAN
It wouldn't make anything better.

DYLAN
Actually, I think you're mistaken about that.

LOGAN
Just finish your food—

GABRIEL
Logan, you gotta chill.

DYLAN
Gabe, did you wash your hands before you touched the plates?

GABRIEL
Yes, but did I mention I rubbed my ass over everything? Aimed a couple of really, really wet farts right at the potatoes.

DYLAN
Logan, do you want my food?

LOGAN
Uh—

DYLAN
Here—

LOGAN
Thanks...

GABRIEL
I keep returning to the thought that nothing is ever going to feel quite right again.

DYLAN
They were two names in a newspaper article, statistics in a headline: fifty dead in bombing—and in a few weeks, they won't even be that, they'll be forgotten entirely.

GABRIEL
Except by us.

DYLAN
But eventually, we'll die too—and then?

GABRIEL
I don't care what happens after I die—

DYLAN
Suit yourself.

LOGAN

It's like a bank-account's been closed.

GABRIEL

"The roses you gave me kept me awake with the sound of their petals falling." That's what Mom said to Dad, after they met.

DYLAN

I wanted to leave, so that this wouldn't happen.

GABRIEL

What's 'this'?

DYLAN

The interrogation of memory.

LOGAN

It's natural—

DYLAN

It's painful for no reason—

GABRIEL

I think I'm starting to see Dylan's side of things.

LOGAN

Then go, both of you. Get the fuck out of here.

GABRIEL

Don't act so hurt…

LOGAN

I'm not hurt, I'm pissed off.

GABRIEL

No, dude, just say you're hurt. That's the truth.

DYLAN

You don't know shit, Gabe. Don't bother pretending like you do. You just come off as clumsy and incompetent.

GABRIEL

Thanks bud.

LOGAN

I have this image of Mom, sitting at the kitchen table, wishing she'd picked warmer floor tiles, shuffling over to the stove to make more hot water; eating a Florida orange or two to keep away a cold; flipping through the pages of a book that used to move her. Did I love this person? I keep asking myself? And did she love me? I can still see her, when she was young, on a summer evening, watching the three of us chase after fireflies. Ankles aching, varicose veins beginning to appear, the neighbors' kids climbing the dogwood tree. She was amazingly beautiful. It crushed me to realize that I hadn't come from her womb. I used to sit on the veranda, in the summer, with her, and listen to the rain strike the tin awnings. And I'd burrow into her arms, and chest, and stomach. And listen. And cry. I probably did that until I was twelve or thirteen.

DYLAN

Pussy.

LOGAN

Shut up.

GABRIEL

Mom told me once that trees were people who found life everlasting.

DYLAN

She wanted a daughter—

LOGAN

She wanted a lot of things.

GABRIEL

Dylan, what are you planning to do with the rest of your life, now that you're rich?

DYLAN

I find that particular question distressing, to be honest.

LOGAN

I think you're a weak person.

DYLAN

Noted.

GABRIEL

Remember last year when we went out to dinner for Mom's birthday? I got so angry at Dad over something he said. I don't remember about what; the what wasn't important—what was important was the battle itself—being in the restaurant, the enclosed space where we could all tear each other apart. What makes me saddest is the memory I have of the waitress's face. She was clearly having a long night, and just wanted to get through her shift...and instead, she had to serve this table of complete fucking lunatics...There was something important in her face; it was a sorrowful face. I bet she'd been waiting tables for thirty years. Same restaurant, same shift. She just wanted to play her role, announce the dinner specials, and go home...and we didn't let her...We kept the whole restaurant open, squabbling...Our family life is was intense—and we hardly realized it. We act normal, but we're not.

LOGAN

We're obsessed with each other—

DYLAN

Unfortunately.

GABRIEL

Iris is gonna be here in a few minutes.

LOGAN

I actually think if I had the choice between beating the shit out of you or Dylan, I'd choose you Gabe—

GABRIEL

Go for it.

LOGAN

Are you afraid of me?

GABRIEL

The blinds are drawn down like eyelids ready for sleep. It's like the house is dreaming us. And no, I'm not afraid of you.

Logan tackles Gabriel and they start to wrestle.

Enter Iris.

IRIS

I knew it. I fucking knew this would happen.

DYLAN
Hello Iris.

IRIS
Hello Dylan. I'm going to sit on the porch for a few minutes and have a cigarette, would you like join me?—while they work things out—

DYLAN
Sure.

Exit Iris and Dylan.

Gabriel and Logan stop wrestling.

LOGAN
That cocksucker.

GABRIEL
Obviously we deserve it.

LOGAN
Yeah.

GABRIEL
It's funny.

LOGAN
Hilarious.

ACT II

Logan and Iris sit a few feet apart.

IRIS
  Dylan's interesting.

LOGAN
  Give me a break.

IRIS
  He is—

LOGAN
  He tries to be—

IRIS
  He's interesting even when he isn't trying to be interesting.

LOGAN
  Whatever you say.

IRIS
  You're jealous of him—

LOGAN
  Whatever you say.

IRIS
  You're all jealous of each other in different ways—it's absurd—

LOGAN
  Whatever you say.

IRIS
  Stop saying that—

LOGAN
  Why are you here?

IRIS
  Because—

LOGAN
  You never respond to my texts—

IRIS
  Look—

LOGAN
  But you respond to Gabe's?

IRIS

We're friends. You and I are not friends.

LOGAN

It really hurts me.

IRIS

Well I'm here. And we're talking. So.

LOGAN

Which makes tonight not about my Mom and Dad. Which sucks.

IRIS

You're being childish.

LOGAN

I'm being honest.

IRIS

I thought it would be nice to see you and to be able to be your friend, but I guess that's not possible.

LOGAN

Is that surprising to you?

IRIS

Who knows.

LOGAN

I've missed you—

IRIS

No, you miss the 17-year old version of me.

LOGAN

That's the only version of you I know.

IRIS

Logan, I have a girlfriend.

LOGAN

What?

IRIS

You heard me.

LOGAN

You date girls now?

IRIS

Sometimes. Does that bother you?

LOGAN

I feel wrecked.

IRIS

Oh stop—

LOGAN

I don't know what to do....

IRIS

I said stop—

LOGAN

Tell me you're kidding.

IRIS

Why would I be kidding?

LOGAN

That's not who you are—

IRIS

Look at me for a second—

LOGAN

I don't want to.

IRIS

Never say something like that to me again—

LOGAN

Like what?

IRIS

Like you own me.

LOGAN

I just can't mentally process the fact that you're here.

IRIS

Yes you can—

LOGAN

You feel slightly unreal: as if none of this is actually happening to me.

IRIS

I assure you: it is—

LOGAN

I tried prayer. Tried writing shit down. Tried going for long runs. Tried meditation. Tried getting shitfaced. Nothing works.

IRIS

Maybe you should stop trying to fix it; maybe it's not something you can fix.

LOGAN

Why didn't you come to the funeral?

IRIS

Because I found out about it too late. My Mom called me this afternoon to tell me what happened; obviously I was shocked—

LOGAN

That strikes me as false.

IRIS

Ok.

LOGAN

What?

IRIS

Yeah, it's false—

LOGAN

So what's the truth?

IRIS

The truth is I chose to skip the funeral because I was afraid to see you and then I felt guilty and texted Gabe.

LOGAN

Thank you.

LOGAN

This is confusing.

IRIS

What is?

LOGAN

Everything.

IRIS

Be more specific—

LOGAN

It's almost two a.m. I can feel the warmth of your body. I'm drunk but I don't feel like I'm drunk. I have a headache. I need to take a shower. I need to sleep. And I'm still so in love with you.

IRIS

First of all, no you're not. Second of all, it was almost a decade ago.

LOGAN

Time is relative.

IRIS

It's not that relative.

LOGAN

I've not had a single healthy relationship since high-school.

IRIS

That's not my problem.

LOGAN

We weren't supposed to break up.

IRIS

That's a creepy thing to say.

LOGAN

I'm afraid of waking up alone tomorrow.

IRIS

I'm sorry—

LOGAN

For what?

IRIS

For what happened to your parents—

LOGAN

I have no idea how to conduct myself in their absence.

IRIS

You have time to figure it out.

LOGAN

I don't think I want to be a lawyer anymore.

IRIS

Then quit.

LOGAN

No, I'll be in the office Monday. I know myself.

IRIS

It's like you want to blame other people for what you don't like
about yourself. Can't have satisfying relationships? That's my
fault. Don't like your career? Your Dad's fault. And so on.

LOGAN

True.

IRIS

So if you can recognize that about yourself, then—

LOGAN
I'm not gonna change—

IRIS
You're frustrating.

LOGAN
I still don't understand what you expected to find...

IRIS
Solid, mature, adult grief.

LOGAN
Welp. Sorry to disappoint you.

IRIS
I didn't say disappointed, I said frustrated—

LOGAN
It makes you feel good, doesn't it?—seeing me so weak—

IRIS
Why would it make me feel good Logan?

LOGAN
It's human nature to take pleasure in other people's suffering.

IRIS
It's not my nature.

LOGAN
I know you still love me—

IRIS
No you don't.

LOGAN
Laying in your parents old station-wagon, our clothes on the floor, the radio on... kissing your inner-thigh... my cock inside you; your voice in my ear, moaning—

IRIS
Yes, thank you for that somewhat accurate description of three inconsequential seconds of our lives.

LOGAN
Doesn't it mean anything to you?

IRIS
I moved on a long time ago: you need to accept that.

LOGAN
You forced yourself to move on—

IRIS

What do you mean 'forced'—

LOGAN

You saw being in love as an impediment—

IRIS

Because it was.

LOGAN

To what?

IRIS

Experience.

LOGAN

What experience?

IRIS

You clearly lack imagination.

LOGAN

What, you wanted to a fuck a bunch of other people?

IRIS

Yeah, that's exactly what I wanted to do. And that's exactly what I did.

LOGAN

Was it worth it?

IRIS

Absolutely.

LOGAN

There's something really joyless about you now—

IRIS

That really pisses me off—

LOGAN

What?

IRIS

You literally cannot see me as anything other than your teenage plaything—

LOGAN

Because you're still really hot—

IRIS

You're a child.

LOGAN

You broke up with me because I disgusted you, deep down.

IRIS

Something like that.

LOGAN

Because it disgusted you how much I turned you on; disgusted by the fact that you could never get enough—

IRIS

I think I've had enough right now.

LOGAN

I can't shake the feeling that this, your being here, is about you and your legacy in this family.

IRIS

I'm sorry if I've offended you. I was genuinely grieving for you and Dylan and Gabe and I genuinely wanted to try to, I dunno, just, make contact; be human.

LOGAN

You're one of the dead to me. So the fact that you're here, only makes me feel like they can come back too.

IRIS

Don't you want to get to know me as I am now?

LOGAN

I want to wake up with you tomorrow. I want to watch you get dressed in the first light.

IRIS

Are you listening to me?

LOGAN

No.

IRIS

Wonderful.

LOGAN

Gabe just wants to fuck you. You know that right?

IRIS

Please stop.

LOGAN

I hate the idea of the two of you hanging out in the city—

IRIS

Stop.

LOGAN

You were the worst thing that happened to me until this week.

IRIS

That's an amazingly stupid thing to say.

LOGAN

Just go upstairs and fuck him and get it over with.

IRIS

Logan: your brother and I are friends; casual friends. We talk maybe eight times a year. We do not fuck. We are not going to fuck.

LOGAN

You do fuck, will fuck again, and the thought is killing me. Literally, killing me.

IRIS

You act like I'm just like this object to be passed back and forth between the two of you—

LOGAN

It just feels like I'm being deceived.

IRIS

You sound manic.

LOGAN

I'm not looking for a diagnosis—

IRIS

What are you looking for then?

LOGAN

I don't know; just not a diagnosis.

IRIS

How much have you had to drink tonight?

LOGAN

Not enough to make things be ok. I'd marry you—

IRIS

Good for you.

LOGAN

I still jack off to you, do you know that? On a regular basis. This morning. Before I'd even knew I'd see you tonight.

IRIS

It's sad to hear you talk like this.

LOGAN

But I want you to know—

IRIS

It just comes off as desperate.

LOGAN

Because I'm desperate.

IRIS

I'm not what you need.

LOGAN

Don't you ever think about me?

IRIS

High-school was fun. But I don't think about it.

LOGAN

I didn't say high-school, I said me.

IRIS

I would think about you Logan, if I knew what to think.

LOGAN

The feeling of skin on skin... God, I miss it.

IRIS

You never really understood my sexuality.

LOGAN

Then you were a very good actor—

IRIS

Yes, I was.

LOGAN

I can still feel the juice squirting down your thighs—

IRIS

I can't believe that we're having this conversation.

LOGAN

What did you expect?

IRIS

I honestly don't know.... Your Dad used to kiss me. Do you know that?

LOGAN

No. I didn't know that.

IRIS

And I used to kiss back. That's why I ended things with you when I did. Because it was too much.

LOGAN

Oh. I see.

IRIS

I need you to know. It didn't go further than that—

LOGAN

No—

IRIS

No?

LOGAN

No Iris. I think what you meant to say is that you had a sexual relationship with my father. When it came time to tell me the truth, just now, you stopped short; you didn't have the balls.

IRIS

I don't expect you to forgive me.

LOGAN

I don't give a shit, honestly. I thought it was Gabe, it turns out to be my Dad—I'm just glad you didn't tell me while he was alive, because I actually would have killed him.

IRIS

I need you to acknowledge my guilt—

LOGAN

Don't touch me.

IRIS

Part of me hates you and your father as if you were a single person—

LOGAN

In a way we are—only half of us is dead now. Like a face half-paralyzed by a stroke.

IRIS

But like, I recognize that you're not the same person, in reality—

LOGAN

Cool, cool—appreciate it—

IRIS

I've never been able to find everything I want in one person—

LOGAN

Other people have such interesting things to say, but it seems so meaningless unaccompanied by pain.

IRIS

You don't think I'm grieving too?

LOGAN

I don't give a shit—

IRIS

I know you feel badly betrayed, but—

LOGAN

Oatmeal. He used to get mad at me for making oatmeal without measuring out the proper ratio of water and oats. My Dad. He used to get so angry. I never understood why. He said it was a metaphor for how I lived my life: not following directions. The irony was that I've spent my entire life following his directions, I'm just not very good at it. Did you think I was boring? Back then?

IRIS

Being seventeen in the suburbs bored me. So I acted out.

LOGAN

As you know, my mother—my step-mother, technically—was suicidal throughout her adult-life, so it was ironic that, in the end, she didn't have to finish the job herself....

IRIS

I was so afraid of your mother. She knew. Without knowing, she knew. And so did you, in a way.

LOGAN

No. Iris. I didn't know. I didn't have a clue.

IRIS

You had plenty of clues—

LOGAN

Like what?

IRIS

The fact that I was unavailable to see you on nights when your father wasn't home. The erratic ways in which your father would behave when you'd have me over. The erratic ways in which I would behave.

LOGAN
It was unimaginable to me—

IRIS
But not to him. And not to me.

LOGAN
You hate me.

IRIS
Why would I be here if I hated you?

LOGAN
Because you want to see me suffer.

IRIS
You don't hurt anyone, you're reliable, you work hard. You're honest.

LOGAN
So fucking what?

IRIS
Why would anyone want to see you suffer?

LOGAN
I don't know. That's what I've been trying to figure out.

LOGAN
The night I blew out my achilles on national television and I texted you and you never texted me back—

IRIS
What about it?

LOGAN
You got that text right?

IRIS
Yes.

LOGAN
And you chose to say nothing in response?

IRIS
Correct.

LOGAN
Why?

IRIS
Why not?

LOGAN

That was my lowest moment.

IRIS

Sure, but it had nothing to with me.

LOGAN

All you had to do was text me back.

IRIS

I felt so much anger. Towards you, towards your father, towards myself.

LOGAN

But I didn't know that.

IRIS

Now you do.

LOGAN

I've felt dizzy for days, my ears have been ringing non-stop.

IRIS

I'm sorry.

LOGAN

What's crazy, is, that more than anything, I just want to have a kid. A son. I want to wake up in the house of my family. More than fear, more than grief, more than anger, there's desire for that, in me.... I used to love getting sick—as a kid—because that's when he'd let up a little and just like, be nice to me. Take me out for ice cream and whatever. It was like, when I was sick, he didn't need me to be perfect anymore.

IRIS

I wish I had a way of chasing the haunted look from your eyes.

LOGAN

At six I wake up, shower, drive to work. Get reamed out by the older attorneys. Then I drive home. Maybe smoke a blunt, watch TV. Then I go to bed. Rinse, repeat. When I got the call telling me they were dead... the thought flashed through my mind: oh good, now I can take two weeks off from work...

IRIS

It's ok—

LOGAN

My reflexes don't work right. You could drive a pin into the palm of my hand and I wouldn't flinch.

IRIS

I want to help you—

LOGAN

I was a sensational athlete. Like, fucking sensational.

IRIS

I remember.

LOGAN

But I've been stripped of my pride, my magnificence, my freedom. My strength.

IRIS

No, it's all there. It's just gone to sleep.

LOGAN

I'm a turnstile, people pass through me on their way to somewhere else—

IRIS

Tell me how I can help you—

LOGAN

A kid with a Teddy-bear. A kid, so full of love. With a little beating heart.

IRIS

I'm not going to bear your children Logan.

LOGAN

I died with my Mom and Dad. I'm just lying in their ashes.

IRIS

You're right here, alive.

LOGAN

A mother brings a child into the world knowing that one day, it has to die—

IRIS

It's an overwhelming responsibility—

LOGAN

So I understand why my first mother gave me up, and why the second couldn't look me in the eye—

IRIS

You've confused love and care-giving...

LOGAN

No, I don't think so.

IRIS
  I don't know what you want me to say.
LOGAN
  I don't either.
IRIS
  Yeah.
LOGAN
  Oh well.
Exit Logan.
Enter Gabriel.
GABRIEL
  Hey.
IRIS
  Hi.
GABRIEL
  I couldn't sleep. You don't look ok—
IRIS
  Well, yeah. I'm not.
GABRIEL
  What happened? What did he say? What did you say?
IRIS
  I don't think I can explain.
GABRIEL
  Try.
IRIS
  It's slipped into the black ooze of memory and it's sinking faster
  than I can swim down and hug it.
GABRIEL
  What is?
IRIS
  Three minutes ago—
GABRIEL
  What did he say, though—specifically—
IRIS
  Something very very private.
GABRIEL
  I see.

IRIS

I'm sorry.

GABRIEL

How did this happen?

IRIS

How did what happen?

GABRIEL

I was the one who said you should come, Logan was the one who said he wanted you to turn around—but we got it backwards: he wanted you here and I wanted you far away.

IRIS

You both want a scapegoat. You tried out Dylan, but he wasn't game, so now it's my turn.

GABRIEL

Iris—

IRIS

You feel ashamed and out of control and you stabilize yourself by beating up on me. And you know it. And you can't bring yourself to say sorry—both of you—

GABRIEL

Fuck me, I'm falling apart.

IRIS

Gabe—

GABRIEL

What?

IRIS

I like it when you smile.

GABRIEL

Sometimes I think about how, if human beings don't wipe themselves out... how in a thousand years, they'll think about how brief life was... and they'll just be in sort of awe at how we didn't go crazy at having to live such short lives.

IRIS

I think people do go crazy though—

GABRIEL

What did Logan say to you?

IRIS
I think the question is, what did I say to him?

GABRIEL
Ok, so—

IRIS
I don't know where to begin.

GABRIEL
Anywhere—

IRIS
I chastised your brother for being obsessed with the past, but I think I'm the one who's obsessed—

GABRIEL
Be specific—

IRIS
I can't.

GABRIEL
Try—

IRIS
I'd sit in your kitchen and have coffee with your mother. Then Logan would drive us to school. That was junior year. I barely saw my own parents; I didn't care. I loved the intimacy of this house.

GABRIEL
Which means what exactly?

IRIS
I don't know. It's just what came to mind.

GABRIEL
What is it that you can't let go of?

IRIS
What won't let go of me—

GABRIEL
Which is what?

IRIS
I don't know.

GABRIEL
You know—

IRIS

I can't believe how much you look like him. It's like you're growing into his face.

GABRIEL

That's an uncomfortable thing to hear.

IRIS

I can't help it.

GABRIEL

Yes you can—

IRIS

I don't want you to be angry with me.

GABRIEL

I'm not angry—

IRIS

What are you then?

GABRIEL

Imperceptibly chilled.

IRIS

That's anger—

GABRIEL

I'm incapable of getting angry.

IRIS

I'm not.

GABRIEL

Good, so you be angry, and I'll just sit here.

IRIS

I didn't say I wanted to, I just said I could.

GABRIEL

When I was maybe like, eight, we went to the wedding of my older cousin, Mike. And um, I just like, danced all night, and people,
said, "look at that crazy kid." I was so happy, I didn't care what
people said—and would I have cared?—I was eight. On the way
back, in the car, I fell asleep, of course. And so did my brothers.
All I remember then, is my Dad carrying me back into the house,
and both of them kissing me goodnight. I still remember how
their skin smelled. And how warm my bed was. How warm my
skin was. How perfect everything seemed.

IRIS

Come here Gabriel—

GABRIEL

I think I'd rather be with them now, wherever they are, than here—

IRIS

Put your head on my shoulder.

GABRIEL

Do you remember last year, when we were at that bar and you asked me to come home with you—

IRIS

Yes.

GABRIEL

You're not used to being told no, are you?

IRIS

No.

GABRIEL

Sorry.

IRIS

I love getting looks from strangers. Love when someone undresses me with their eyes. That's when my boredom is alleviated. That's when I light up. That's what happens when you're brought up taking ballet lessons, singing lessons, gymnastics, cheerleading— when you're systematically trained to seek applause, recognition, approval—

GABRIEL

I didn't want to reduce you to my desire for you—

IRIS

You don't have to justify yourself—

GABRIEL

Your pride was wounded—

IRIS

Who cares about my pride?

GABRIEL

I do.

IRIS

Why?

GABRIEL

Because people who have pride are less of a burden on me than those who don't.

IRIS

Playing on peoples' fantasies is the way I get power over them, so when I can't do that, I don't know what to do.

GABRIEL

Why is power necessary?

IRIS

Because: what do you replace power with?

GABRIEL

I wish I were more comfortable with being sincere.

IRIS

Me too.

GABRIEL

Because I feel sincere. You know. It's just hard to be the way I feel.

IRIS

What will I do when I stop being beautiful? I need someone to tell me.

GABRIEL

Iris, don't be an idiot—

IRIS

Your voice is so gentle. Even when you're being critical. Everything about you is gentle. And kind.

GABRIEL

It's a method of coping.

IRIS

What's wrong with me?

GABRIEL

Nothing.

IRIS

I constantly obsess over my own desirability.

GABRIEL

What does that accomplish?

IRIS

It's just what I do.

GABRIEL

My parents were successful participants in a consumer society. They made money. They lived comfortably. And so they assumed that they had figured things out. Arrogant fucks. They died full of self-hatred and confusion—

IRIS

And you think I will too...

GABRIEL

We're supposed to get wiser with age—but we don't, I don't think.

IRIS

You say you don't get angry, but—

GABRIEL

Something's torn open inside of me.

IRIS

Maybe you should punch a pillow or something.

GABRIEL

No.

IRIS

I wish I had met you independent of your family? Outside of everything. In another life—

GABRIEL

Iris—

IRIS

What?

GABRIEL

We can't change our circumstances.

IRIS

It's freezing in here.

GABRIEL

Do you want me to get you a sweatshirt?

IRIS

No, that's ok.

GABRIEL

Are you sure?

IRIS

Can you put your arms around me?

GABRIEL

Let's just not talk or look at each other for a second.

IRIS

Am I embarrassing you?

GABRIEL

Yes.

IRIS

I feel like anything is possible tonight.

GABRIEL

Maybe, but that doesn't mean it should be—you know?

IRIS

Yeah. I know.

GABRIEL

There were no bodies. At the funeral. That's what I can't get over: the absence of a corpses; of any sign that the bodies I called my parents used to exist.

IRIS

Gabe, I understand how difficult this is—

GABRIEL

Do you?

IRIS

No.

GABRIEL

Then why would you say you do?

IRIS

Because that's the socialized response.

GABRIEL

Exactly.

IRIS

Am I required to have something more than platitudes right now?

GABRIEL

No, you're not.

IRIS

So give me a break.

GABRIEL

I just didn't know you were going to show up here expecting sympathy from us.

IRIS

Excuse me?

GABRIEL

Never mind.

IRIS

Why did you say it was ok for me to come over if you harbored all
this resentment towards me?

GABRIEL

I don't harbor resentment towards you—

IRIS

It sure seems like—

GABRIEL

I can't focus on anything. I keep reaching for my phone as if
they're gonna text me and tell me they're still. I've been having a
quiet panic attack since I turned on my phone and saw there was a
bombing at the same hotel—

IRIS

Take a deep breath.

GABRIEL

The funeral was disgusting. People come, pay their respects,
pretend to say a prayer, go home. And that's it. Today I shook
hands with several hundred people who don't actually give a fuck.
And in turn, when those people die, hundreds more people will
attend those funerals just because that's what they believe they're
supposed to do. And maybe the worst thing about it was the social
aspect: golf buddies catching up, old ladies gossiping, second
cousins flirting with each other. It was a day at the country club,
not a funeral.

IRIS

You should have stood up and said something—

GABRIEL

No, I'm too gutless—

IRIS

Bullcrap.

GABRIEL

That's the point of this whole conversation, Iris. I'm the safe one.
The nice one. The one who never does anything. You have all
the power here. You want to fuck me—then fuck me. You think

I have self-control? No no no no no. I've got self-pity, self-loath-
ing. Self-control? Self-control would mean being able to kiss you,
because that's what I want to do. But I can't because I won't.

IRIS

Wrong answer.

GABRIEL

I wonder what it was like, in the fifteen seconds between the
terror and the explosion.... Gun shots. Screams. Then, bang: and
time stands still.

IRIS

I think it's still frozen.

GABRIEL

I'm chasing after the dead, trying to call them back. But they can't
hear me, so they don't turn around.

IRIS

Gabe: I don't want you to die. Ok?

GABRIEL

Iris: who said I'm gonna die?

IRIS

I just had this terrible premonition.

GABRIEL

Of what?

IRIS

I just really care about your life. I want you to know that.

GABRIEL

Where is this coming from?

IRIS

It's so beautiful: to feel my heart beating like this.

GABRIEL

I tried watching some home videos this morning, but I had to
stop.

IRIS

Can you kiss my neck?

GABRIEL

My whole life, I've been torn between Logan, who did everything
my father asked, and Dylan, who did the opposite of everything
my father asked.

IRIS

There's something sane, I think, in avoiding extremes.

GABRIEL

I don't feel very sane.

IRIS

You will. Because you are.

GABRIEL

I never understood why my father stayed with my mother.

IRIS

What didn't you understand?

GABRIEL

How he endured her.

IRIS

The same way you endured him—

GABRIEL

Before I came down here, I looked out my window and watched the geese, high up in the moonlight.... And um... I think I'm gonna quit acting.

IRIS

Idiot.

GABRIEL

I can hear my Dad's voice in my brothers. It's crushing. Telling me that I'm not good enough—

IRIS

It's just like the funeral: why don't you say something? Stand up for yourself?

GABRIEL

I think I'd rather quietly cut them out of my life.

IRIS

Why do you act weaker than you really are?

GABRIEL

Because what's the point of being strong? What did it get Logan, and his own way—what does it get Dylan?

IRIS

I don't know.

GABRIEL

Fuck expectations. Fuck being exceptional, it's an addiction. I
don't need that shit.

IRIS

Are you sure?

GABRIEL

Maybe I should become a Buddhist—

IRIS

It's better to bloom late, then never at all—

GABRIEL

Why do you care about me?

IRIS

Isn't it obvious?

GABRIEL

No.

IRIS

You look so much like your father, it's almost disturbing.

GABRIEL

You've already alluded to that fact.

IRIS

But I can't get over it.

GABRIEL

Children are vessels for genes to survive in.

IRIS

That's one way to put it.

GABRIEL

When I first got back, I laid down in the backyard for a while,
smelled the damp of the oak leaves, felt how the mud grips their
absence.

IRIS

I want to know you Gabriel—

GABRIEL

Everywhere life is deeper, more beautiful that I can describe.

IRIS

I want to know who you are—

GABRIEL

It's grief not just for them, but everything that surrounded them:

the smell of lilacs in the garden after a long rain, soup simmering in the kitchen.

IRIS

I don't know what I'll do if you don't let me into your life.

GABRIEL

Spiritual pain. It has its own tongue, its own vocal chords. All day I've just wanted to scream.

IRIS

Then scream.

GABRIEL

No.

IRIS

Scream Gabe—

GABRIEL

No.

IRIS

Do it—

GABRIEL

No—

IRIS

Come on—

GABRIEL

No—

IRIS

Don't be a bitch—

GABRIEL

You can have my bed, I'll take the couch.

IRIS

You're going to sleep?

GABRIEL

Yeah.

IRIS

I'm not ready for this conversation to be over.

GABRIEL

It never started.

IRIS

You should have your own bed tonight. The couch is fine for me.

GABRIEL

  Are you sure?

IRIS

  Yeah, I'm sure.

GABRIEL

  I'll get you a blanket.

IRIS

  Thanks.

Exit Gabriel.

Gabriel returns with a blanket and a glass of water.

GABRIEL

  Here ya go.

IRIS

  Thanks.

GABRIEL

  You're welcome.

IRIS

  I feel like a small bird that keeps dashing itself against the window—

GABRIEL

  Goodnight Iris.

IRIS

  G'night Gabe.

GABRIEL

  The dead blind us on their way out. So we have to rely on new senses. New intuitions.

IRIS

  I guess I'll see you in the morning—

GABRIEL

  Ok. Yeah. See you.

Exit Gabriel.

Dawn.

Iris is asleep.

Enter Dylan.

IRIS

  Hey.

DYLAN

   Sorry to wake you, I didn't realize you were down here—

IRIS

   I don't mind.

DYLAN

   Are you sure?

IRIS

   Yes. I enjoyed our little chat on the porch last night.

DYLAN

   So did I.

IRIS

   You're a very insightful person.

DYLAN

   I just say shit. Do you want coffee? I just made some.

IRIS

   Yes please.

DYLAN

   Ok. I'll be right back.

Exit Dylan.

Dylan returns with two cups of coffee.

IRIS

   Thanks.

DYLAN

   You're welcome.

IRIS

   I feel sheepish.

DYLAN

   Why?

IRIS

   Because I told myself that I was coming here to help you guys, and I immediately became a burden.

DYLAN

   That's just how it works.

IRIS

   That's just how what works exactly?

DYLAN

   A savior complex.

IRIS

You think I have a savior complex?

DYLAN

No, I think you're hiding other complexes beneath a savior complex.

IRIS

Fun.

DYLAN

Well.

IRIS

Yeah. Dylan—

DYLAN

Sup?

IRIS

I'm really in love with the person I'm dating. Her name is Ava. I don't know why I'm bringing that up all of a sudden—

DYLAN

Ava's a nice name.

IRIS

I called her like three times on the drive up last night. She didn't pick up. And after everyone went to bed, I called her again. I don't know why.

DYLAN

Do you want to talk about it?

IRIS

I sound idiotic.

DYLAN

How long have you been seeing her?

IRIS

Like two months.

DYLAN

I see.

IRIS

I don't think I'm actually in love with her. I think I'm just infatuated. I think I just like the game aspect.

It's not appropriate to think like that, I know—

DYLAN
Thoughts aren't supposed to be appropriate—
IRIS
Then what are they supposed to be?
DYLAN
Clear.
IRIS
But clear is cruel—
DYLAN
But at least you know where you stand with cruelty—
IRIS
I'm not the same person I was before I fell asleep I don't think.
DYLAN
Why?
IRIS
I've recognized something in myself that I don't care for.
DYLAN
A pity. Are you going back to the city, or are you gonna hang here today?
IRIS
Are you trying to get rid of me?
DYLAN
No.
IRIS
You're trying to get rid of me!
DYLAN
No, Iris, that's not what I'm doing.
IRIS
Now I feel insecure.
DYLAN
You don't know what you're feeling.
IRIS
Excuse me?
DYLAN
I said: you don't know what you're feeling.
IRIS
You're probably right.

DYLAN

But you should.

IRIS

Oh yeah?

DYLAN

It's irresponsible to be here otherwise.

IRIS

Do you know what you're feeling Dylan?

DYLAN

Nothing out of the ordinary. Today's begun, life continues. I'm
hungry, I have to take a shit. My flight leaves at five.

IRIS

I appreciate you Dylan—

DYLAN

I'm uncomfortable with compliments. I don't see what they accomplish.

IRIS

They make you feel good.

DYLAN

I don't want to feel good.

IRIS

Why did you become a famous entrepreneur then?

DYLAN

I'm not famous—

IRIS

You're not not famous—

DYLAN

My business is famous; I'm not. I'm outside the frame.

IRIS

People know your name.

DYLAN

People know my brand.

IRIS

That's like, the definition of fame.

DYLAN

That's the definition of selling your soul.

IRIS

With the other two, they pretend to hide their feelings, but they're always letting me know exactly what's going on; with you, it's different.

DYLAN

I think you want to come away from this trip with some kind of special snowflake memory, and you've decided it's me—

IRIS

Maybe I'm trying to build you up into something. Yeah. I don't know.

DYLAN

Do you want some pancakes or something? Buckwheat pancakes, with cinnamon powder. That's what my Mom used to make. I'm not sure if I could make them as well as she did, but I could try?

IRIS

Maybe in a little bit. Thanks.

DYLAN

I've been thinking that I want to give my money away to charity.

IRIS

Will that make you happy?

DYLAN

It'll make someone happy—

IRIS

But you—

DYLAN

I'll be the same. I'm always the same—

IRIS

Which is what?

DYLAN

As a little kid, I had great difficulty speaking. I was mostly silent until I was ten or eleven.

IRIS

What made you want to talk to other people—

DYLAN

I was curious to see if they were as interesting as my dreams were.

IRIS

And were they?

DYLAN
Sometimes yes, sometimes no. More no than yes.

IRIS
Why are you looking at me like that?

DYLAN
Because behind each face, there is another and another and another—

IRIS
So what?

DYLAN
You cheated on Logan a bunch in high-school—

IRIS
How do you know that?

DYLAN
I just paid attention. It was written on your face, on the faces of the dudes that you were fucking.... I was so small and insignificant, you know? No one noticed I was even there, in the hallways and stuff. And people brag. But who cares? What does fidelity matter when you're seventeen?

IRIS
Or ever.

DYLAN
Or ever. Just look at my father.

IRIS
What exactly are you referring to Dylan?

DYLAN
You know exactly what I'm referring to. It was pretty funny. I always had to remove the hotel bills from my Dad's pockets when he got back from seeing you. It was really like he was trying to get caught.

IRIS
I'm sure he was.

DYLAN
And I resented having to work so hard to keep my mother from finding out—

IRIS
I'm sorry I put you in that position.

DYLAN

You're not sorry—

IRIS

I need to get the fuck out of here. It's got me all fucked up and confused being back in this house. Suddenly I feel like I'm a teenager again and just as passive and stupidly vulnerable as I was then and it's not fair—

DYLAN

It's perfectly fair.

IRIS

What exactly are you trying to prove?

DYLAN

Good question.

IRIS

I shouldn't have ignored you, when you were a kid. I didn't know how to be your friend—

DYLAN

You still don't—

IRIS

Tell me: what should I do, what should I say?

DYLAN

You know, once you've learned to overhear yourself—once you've learned to catch the brain as it leaps from the tongue—you can begin to invent who you are. And re-invent and re-invent and re-invent—

IRIS

Last night I dreamed three flowers bloomed: one in my head, one in my heart, and one in the palm of my hand.

DYLAN

Am I supposed to interpret that?

IRIS

I feel like you really understand people—

DYLAN

I don't understand anything about anyone—

IRIS

You understand too well—

DYLAN

No really Iris: I live in a state of very deep, spiritual indifference in which I can't really see into people, only see the ways in which I can slide them back and forth across the chess board.

IRIS

Do you think I'm any different?

DYLAN

No. Probably not.

IRIS

But what if I am different? And what if you are too?

DYLAN

I think God is probably astonished when He receives souls in heaven; astonished at the wounds they bear—

IRIS

You didn't answer my question—

DYLAN

I have this app that helps me meditate. It's just like, white static noise and this dude talking calmly. I put it on and imagine that I'm just a brain floating in a vat.

IRIS

You're suffering—

DYLAN

I can't fucking handle it Iris. To be honest.

IRIS

Dylan...

DYLAN

How did things end up like this? How did I get from there to here—from my mother's arms—to here—this abandoned place?

IRIS

I don't know.

DYLAN

When someone dies, suddenly you're deprived of all the things you were saving for the right moment to say to them.

IRIS

What did you want to say to them?

DYLAN

Probably just thank you, because while they could have been better, they also could have been worse.

IRIS

I see.

DYLAN

We're all self-creating, self-deepening, unbearably melancholy
creatures. And I wish I understood why—

IRIS

Do you ever become so aware of your own heartbeat that you start
to feel that if you stop being aware, your heart will actually stop?

DYLAN

Sometimes—

IRIS

I guess I'm thinking about what you said about moving people
around like chess pieces—

DYLAN

Good.

IRIS

Are you doing that right now?

DYLAN

Sometimes I feel like I'm floating in a hot-air balloon, looking
down.

IRIS

I could be at home, in bed, asleep right now.

DYLAN

That's true.

IRIS

So why am I not doing that?

DYLAN

You tell me—

IRIS

Sometimes I get home from my work, to my little shitty studio
apartment and I just basically like fall onto the floor and couch
and start bawling. I don't feel like I have any real interactions with
anyone. And I'm desperate not to feel that way anymore. Which
is why I'm here. Fundamentally. Because at least it feels real. I'll
take real at any cost, at this point.

DYLAN
  Makes sense.
IRIS
  Does it?
DYLAN
  Sure. Why not?
IRIS
  I still associate autumn with high-school. I can still feel your
  brother's lips pressed against my neck at the homecoming dance,
  and the smell of flowers from his lapel, and his hand on the small
  of my back. I'm not even sure if I like sleeping with men, but the
  memories are nice because they're from a time when everything
  seemed like it made sense. Have you ever let a man fuck you
  Dylan?
DYLAN
  Once, at a party.
IRIS
  Did you like it?
DYLAN
  No.
IRIS
  You surprise me.
DYLAN
  Whatever.
IRIS
  I don't know what I'm supposed to say next—
DYLAN
  I'm worried about going bald. I spend thirty minutes each morn-
  ing combing my hair, looking to see how much hair gets caught in
  the brush.
IRIS
  But you're not going bald...
DYLAN
  Oh no, absolutely not, but it worries me anyway.
IRIS
  So...

DYLAN

And I get out of bed to check to see if I left the fridge door open at least five times every night because I'm afraid of letting all the cold air out, but of course—it's always properly shut—

IRIS

Ok, I see where you're going with this—

DYLAN

And I have to cross the street in exactly five seconds every time and if I take too long or go too fast, I cross the street again and again until I get it right.

IRIS

Right right right: I get the picture.

DYLAN

You said you associate autumn with the high-school, and so do I; but for me, that meant getting pushed into lockers and being called a faggot—

IRIS

I didn't realize...

DYLAN

Yes you did—

IRIS

No, really I didn't—

DYLAN

I specifically remember you watching me and doing nothing about it, as if I didn't exist.

IRIS

Is that why you're punishing me right now?

DYLAN

I don't give a fuck about what happened in high-school—

IRIS

Yes you do—

DYLAN

I bought a gun, I made plans to shoot up the whole school.

IRIS

Oh Dylan, no... please say you didn't—

DYLAN

Don't worry, I buried the gun in a field and disavowed violence.

IRIS

Is that the absolute truth?

DYLAN

I hope so.

IRIS

This is really bad—

DYLAN

So I think I understood the terrorist; I think I understood what
was in his heart—

IRIS

You don't mean that—

DYLAN

Why wouldn't I?

IRIS

Because you don't.

DYLAN

Deprived of proper affection, people explode, like stars at the end
of a life cycle. You were one of the people I planned to shoot—

IRIS

I assumed as much.

DYLAN

In case it wasn't clear.

IRIS

I feel unwell.

DYLAN

I promised myself when you arrived, that, by morning, I'd make
you feel what I've felt my whole life.

IRIS

Which is what?

DYLAN

Insignificance.

IRIS

I think that I'm in shock.

DYLAN

Also. Question. What if I didn't bury the gun in a field? What if I
hid it somewhere in the house?

IRIS

Then I would feel very unsafe.

DYLAN

And what if I told you that when I walk out of this room, you'll
soon after hear the sound of a bullet passing through my brain?
Or alternatively: the brains of my brothers—

IRIS

That's not going to happen—

DYLAN

How do you know?

IRIS

Because it just can't.

DYLAN

Is it possible that there's a fourth, static dimension of time apart
from the past, present, and future? Something like perfect time?
I've always wondered—

IRIS

Please sit down.

DYLAN

I'd rather keep pacing.

IRIS

I want Logan and Gabe to come down here.

DYLAN

You have to understand that I'm jealous of the person who can
strap a bomb to their chest and find meaning through martyrdom:
it takes tremendous courage.

IRIS

No it doesn't.

DYLAN

It's funny, I feel nostalgia for people and places that were nothing
to me, but I don't feel anything the people who were everything.

IRIS

I don't believe there's a gun—

DYLAN

But your hands are shaking—

IRIS

And they're not gonna stop for a long time.

DYLAN

Maybe that's the point.

IRIS

I don't want to die.

DYLAN

You could just shout for my brothers to come running in here and pin me to the floor, and they would. Or you could just tackle me. I'm not particularly strong.

IRIS

Is there a gun in this house?

DYLAN

I forget.

IRIS

I don't like that your eyes are scanning the room—

DYLAN

Spiritual thirst. You have to dig a well just like you have to dig a grave. Which is what God wants, I think: for us to dig our graves like we're digging for water.

IRIS

Who do you love Dylan? I need to know—

DYLAN

The most important thing a mother can do, is sing a lullaby to their children. They'll never forget it.

IRIS

I can't bring myself to say his name. Your father's name. I keep swallowing the first syllable like I'm gasping for air.

DYLAN

It never ended, did it?

IRIS

No, I saw him two weeks ago.

DYLAN

Figures.

IRIS

Where are you going?

DYLAN

Upstairs.

IRIS
  I don't want you to do that—
DYLAN
  I know you don't—
IRIS
  Please—
DYLAN
  You're over-thinking it—
IRIS
  Please—
DYLAN
  I'm sorry.
  Exit Dylan.

FIN.

www.ingramcontent.com/pod-product-compliance
Lightning Source LLC
LaVergne TN
LVHW041235080426
835508LV00011B/1222